PUPPIES

Other titles in the series

Keeping and Caring for Your Pet

Fish: Keeping and Caring for Your Pet
Library Edition ISBN 978-0-7660-4185-1
Paperback ISBN 978-1-4644-0301-9

Guinea Pigs: Keeping and Caring for Your Pet
Library Edition ISBN 978-0-7660-4184-4
Paperback ISBN 978-1-4644-0299-9

Kittens: Keeping and Caring for Your Pet
Library Edition ISBN 978-0-7660-4186-8
Paperback ISBN 978-1-4644-0303-3

Rabbits: Keeping and Caring for Your Pet
Library Edition ISBN 978-0-7660-4183-7
Paperback ISBN 978-1-4644-0297-5

PUPPIES

Keeping and Caring for Your Pet

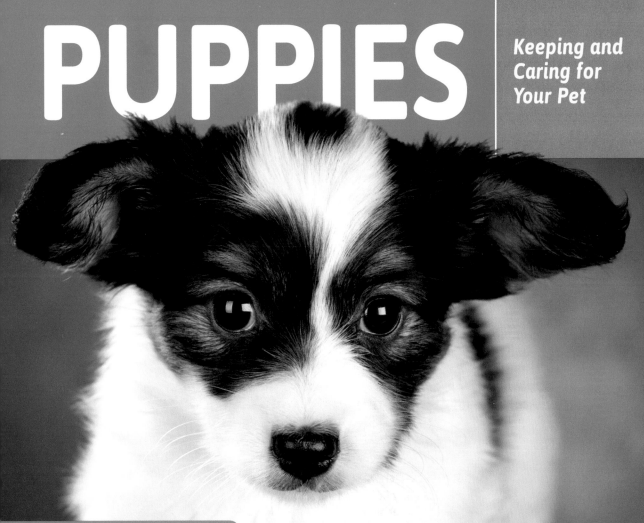

Brigitte Harries

E | **Enslow Publishers, Inc.**

40 Industrial Road
Box 398
Berkeley Heights, NJ 07922
USA

http://www.enslow.com

Contents

3

2

1

Choosing and Bringing Home a Puppy

Ready for a Puppy?
Your New Dog

So you have decided you would like to get a dog. Perhaps you think a dog will make a great addition to your family. You can have a new friend to spend time with. Maybe you believe a dog will make your life better and make you happy. She certainly can, but this works both ways. You need to give your dog plenty of time and attention and work hard to understand her. Then, she in turn will do her best to make you happy.

This puppy seeks security by staying close to her owner.

What Dogs Really Want

The most important thing in your dog's life is you. She needs your care and wants to be your constant companion. She will have complete trust in you right from the beginning, so make sure you do your best to never let her down.

Loyal to You

Your dog is bound to show an interest in other dogs when she is out walking. But she will always come right back to you because she considers you a part of her pack, and a dog never leaves her pack.

Is There Enough Room in Your Pack?

As a responsible owner, you should only invite a dog to be a member of your pack if you are willing to look after her and take her special talents and interests seriously. You will be viewed as pack leader by your dog.

Could You Love an Underdog?

Perhaps you want to take your dog to agility classes or something similar. You may be so excited about this idea that you have not considered the possibility that your dog may not be suited to this, for whatever reason. Will you still want to keep your dog if she does not measure up to your expectations?

Dogs and children can make a great team when they grow up and play together.

→ Unconditional Love

A dog will love her humans unconditionally. It does not matter whether we are rich or poor, pretty or ugly, old or young. A dog will never judge her owner.

A Good Chance in Life

If you willingly take on the responsibility of owning and caring for a dog, then she has a chance of living a good life and becoming a beloved member of the family. The many thousands of abandoned dogs in shelters say it all: in the human-dog relationship, it is the human that gives up—not the dog.

Are You Ready for a Puppy? **Test**

Answer the following questions honestly and to the best of your knowledge:

☐ Will I be able to give my dog all the exercise she needs?

☐ Can I help her foster her natural skills (e.g., swimming, running, tracking)?

☐ Will I have the strength to restrain her in a difficult situation?

☐ Is her size suitable for me and my family? (Because younger siblings may also want to walk her on the leash.)

☐ Can my family and I deal with the shedding all around the house?

☐ Am I willing to give my dog the correct care, according to her breed?

☐ Will she fit in my family's car?

☐ Does my family have enough money for everyday costs, such as food, insurance, vet bills, and vaccinations?

☐ Are my family members free from allergies?

If you answered "yes" to all the questions, you are ready for a puppy! Consider your local animal shelter before going to a breeder.

A house with a fenced-in yard is ideal for a dog; she can run around and play freely.

Some people suffer from allergies caused by environmental allergens, which unfortunately means they may also develop an allergic reaction to dogs (saliva, animal dander, and fur).

The ideal home for your dog depends on her breed. Small dogs do not need that much room and may do just fine in an apartment or small house. But larger dogs do better in an average-sized home with a yard that does not require too much care. It is likely that your dog will mess up your yard when she is digging and playing. Be sure to protect any flower or vegetable gardens from your dog. If you live near woods or trailways, you can take your dog for long walks near your home.

Dog Friendly Neighborhood?

If your dog barks a lot, she is bound to upset the neighbors. You need to take this into consideration. If you live in a rented house or apartment building, check with your landlord whether a dog is allowed. Find out if getting a dog would upset anyone in your building. Someone could be allergic or have a fear of dogs. Dogs that are not in any way disruptive should not be a problem. But be careful. A judge will often rule against a dog owner if the animal is problematic in any way.

Dogs and the Law

You will save yourself a lot of trouble if you take time to inform yourself about dogs and the law right from the beginning. Make sure you find out what the laws concerning dogs are in your state and also your local area. These may include licenses, the number of dogs you can keep, vaccinations, areas which are off-limits to dogs, dog waste disposal, dogs in cars, animal burial restrictions, which breeds are classified as dangerous, and also what the restraint requirements are, such as a muzzle and walking your dog on the leash. Some rules make life more difficult when it comes to the ownership of your dog: higher taxes and house insurance premiums, a dog ban in your apartment, dogs not allowed on public transportation, and other issues.

A Dog Will Take Up a Lot of Your Time

Before you get your new dog, make a diary of your daily activities and think how you could fit in caring for a dog on top of this. Would you have enough time? If so, would you be happy to spend a lot of this spare time walking her, training her, and playing with her before you collapse on the sofa at the end of a busy day?

The Problem With Vacations

Taking your dog with you on vacation could be very restrictive. Your favorite time of the year could be a huge ordeal for your dog. The best solution is to leave her with trustworthy friends who are experienced in looking after dogs.

Dog Sitters

You will probably need at least three willing dog sitters in your circle of friends, who will have time to look after your dog when you go away. Even the most well-run kennels can be very stressful for a dog. A kennel that promises happy days for your dog can sometimes be misleading. No dog will be relaxed and happy when separated from her owner. She will not understand where you have gone and whether you are coming back. On the other hand, it is not a good idea to take her away with you because the journey could be very stressful, for example being kept in a transportation cage on a plane.

If you must take your dog on vacation with you, make sure the journey is safe, and she is made to feel welcome at the destination.

Young dogs in particular can get into all sorts of mischief. Your well-kept lawn could soon be destroyed!

→ Not Sure?

Perhaps you got a sinking feeling when you read these points above? Then it is possible that a dog is not right for you. It may be better for you to get a cat, or you may need to change a few things about your lifestyle before you are ready to get a dog. It may be best to wait until the time is right for you before making such a big commitment.

The Best Dog for You

Dogs accept us and love us just as we are. Sadly, all too often, dogs are treated by humans as material possessions, as something that we humans own. A human should love his or her dog for better or worse, but unfortunately, the dog sometimes comes off worse and ends up in a shelter.

Think hard about what type of dog you would like: a crossbred dog with messy, curly fur; a streamlined, muscular athletic type; an elegant dog with a silky coat; a huge softie with an aristocratic flair; a tiny, sprightly dog; or a gentle giant . . . the possibilities are endless!

Pedigree or Mixed-Breed?

There are many different breeds in addition to various hybrids for you to choose from. There are lots of books that outline the different breeds using photos and plenty of information for you to read. These are useful as a first reference, but the best thing to do is to get to know a dog from your favorite breed—not just cute little puppies but also adult dogs, so you can see what he will be like when he is older! You could contact kennel clubs and breeder clubs or dog training schools for more information. Perhaps you could go on a few walks with this particular type of dog and observe him carefully. What is his temperament like? How does he behave with other dogs? And young children? Do you like to hear his bark or do you find it annoying?

Big or Small?

What may initially appear as an elegant dog stretched out on the lawn could become a bull in a china shop when indoors, especially large and active breeds. If you know

Whether pedigree or mixed-breed, lapdog or gentle giant, consider not only the appearance but the nature of the breed as well.

The Parson Russell terrier is a playful little dog with an irresistible charm.

The German shepherd is still one of the most popular breeds. He is a good watchdog and needs plenty to keep him busy.

someone who owns the breed you like, you could visit him in his home or even better, invite the owner to your house with the dog. Is he too big for your home?

That Wet Dog Smell

Have you ever smelled that strong odor after a dog has been walking in the rain or swimming? It is okay when he is outdoors, but once you get him inside your home, you may find the smell unbearable. Also, you may already have noticed that there is more to your dog than just his appearance. Every adult dog still likes to play and will need consistent training, so it makes sense to find out about behavior that is typical of each breed you are interested in. If this sounds like too much work, then perhaps a dog is not for you.

You Are His Life

Perhaps for you, a dog is just one of the many important things in your life, but for your dog, you are his dependable companion forever. You should spend time getting to know the characteristics of a specific breed before you make a decision as to whether that dog is right for you.

You will be a team for many years to come. In the case of hybrid dog breeds, for example, Labradoodles, find out the main information for both breeds.

Male or Female?

It is possible that before you even go to see a litter of puppies, you may have an idea whether you would prefer to have a male or a female.

→ Males are often stronger and rowdier. They are also more likely to show you their dominant side. They are often larger and may display sexual urges, such as humping your leg.

→ Females are often more delicate and easier to train than males. You will need to take extra care when they are in heat (twice a year for about three weeks at a time). She may become lethargic and listless if she has a pseudopregnancy, which means she might show signs of being pregnant when in fact, she is not. In the case of larger breeds, it would probably be best to get a female if you are inexperienced. But bear in mind that spaying a female dog is a more complex operation than neutering a male.

Left: Springer spaniels have a friendly nature and enjoy scent-tracking.

Above: Breeds such as golden retrievers and Labrador retrievers have become very popular family dogs over the years.

→ What Is a Puppy Test?

Breeders sometimes carry out tests on their puppies, which involves asking a person who has never met the puppies to interact with them, in order to learn how each one reacts in certain situations. This is a good way to find out how curious a puppy is and whether he is self-confident, dominant, or submissive.

*There Is No Such Thing as
the Perfect Family Dog*

No Refunds Allowed

Over the last couple of decades, the idea of a perfect family dog came into vogue, and if you were to see advertisements for such dogs, you would probably be very tempted to get one. However, a dog from family dog advertising laundry detergent or toilet paper is all very well, but do not forget that although you can change your brand of toilet paper, your dog will be with you for ten or fifteen years!

The ideal family dog is one that responds well to people, plays nicely with children without showing aggression, and enjoys being stroked and cuddled.

any breed can become the "ideal" family dog, so make sure you do your research before you make a decision. Only you know which breed of dog would suit your family best.

Misleading Advertising

Those who blindly trusted that the family dogs shown in advertisements on the television were perfect may have spent many years regretting this. A perfect

Good Watchdog

One type of family dog that often appears an attractive option is the watchdog, a loyal animal that courageously guards his family and defends it against the dangers of the world. But some overprotective watchdogs will not let visitors in or out! A dog who loves his owners is great, but if he is the one who decides who is and is not allowed into the house, life could get pretty lonely.

Jack of All Trades

This family dog (below) is energetic, down-to-earth, playful, and loves to get involved in the action. Also, he is an appropriate size for small children and will love to play with them—the livelier the game, the better. On the other hand, his feisty nature may mean he fights with other dogs, whether they are small or large, and he may be tempted to stray off the path whenever he finds an interesting scent.

Gentle Giant

Another option is a gentle giant, such as a Great Dane or Saint Bernard. These good-natured fellows will not usually lose their temper or protest whenever your little brother or sister climbs all over them. However, small children should not be left alone with large dogs, or any dog for that matter, because accidents do happen. Also, large dog breeds tend not to be as excitable as smaller dogs and can be difficult to motivate.

→ Dogs in Fashion

Retrievers have long been rightly regarded as the ideal family dog. However, since their popularity has spread like wildfire, sadly, they have been bred irresponsibly, which has meant their health has suffered and their nature has gone to the dogs, so to speak. Many end up in shelters because they are still dogs after all, and every dog needs consistent training. Choosing a dog breed because it is in fashion, without actually knowing anything about the dog itself, can soon end in disaster: border collies need constant attention; sled dogs, such as the Siberian husky or Alaskan malamute, want to run long distances and cannot tolerate the heat; West Highland white terriers, or Westies, have skin problems; Jack Russell terriers are hunting dogs and may chase anything that moves; and Bernese mountain dogs often have problems with their joints. These are all points you will need to consider when choosing a breed.

True Humanitarians

An ideal family dog is a dog that loves and trusts all people and even greets strangers in a friendly manner, and he remains playful well into old age. This is a dog with serenity and self-confidence, that tolerates and loves even the noisiest, most excitable toddlers. He sees "his" children as playmates and best friends and enjoys being cuddled and fussed over.

Identify His Needs

Keep in mind that each breed description is more or less an over-embellished advertisement for a particular breed. Many breeders who are passionate about a certain breed will be blind to its faults. Do not convince yourself that you can train him out of these faults. Just as every breed has a genetically programmed appearance, it also has ingrained behaviors as well.

EXTRA
Dog Advertisements

What They Really Mean

Please make sure that you do not fall into the trap of buying your dog from a cleverly disguised dog trader. Modern dog dealers often disguise their companies as dog shelters or dog kennels in order to attract trusting animal lovers. Keep in mind that in real animal shelters, there are usually more older animals than there are puppies.

What the Ads Reveal

Immoral Traders

Dogs from the breeder: long-haired dachshunds, cocker spaniels of all colors, toy poodles, collies, Dobermans, Saint Bernards, boxers, Irish setters, German shepherds and many more breeds, healthy and well-cared-for animals . . .

This ad is an example of a puppy mill, where puppies are mass-produced for a profit. Puppies are bred and kept in cages, crates, or old pigsties without formative, positive human experiences to enrich their lives. Almost inevitably, this causes the animals mental and physical health problems. Never support this type of animal cruelty by buying one of these puppies. For every puppy you rescue, there will be another in its place.

Fashionable Dog Breeds

White golden retriever, female, 1 yr, from class A1 breed, to be sold to the very best owner, telephone Sunday from 5 P.M.

Some dog breeders only breed the most fashionable dogs in order to make the most profit.

Making a Quick Buck

Pedigree boxer puppies, without papers, telephone . . .

If the puppies are indeed pedigree, a reputable breeder would have the documents proving this. Perhaps the seller's dog became pregnant accidentally and the seller is taking advantage of the situation to make money, or maybe the dog was purposely bred for profit. There is also the possibility that the puppies could have been stolen.

Dog Traders

Perfect Puppies
Daily veterinary health care, vaccinated and dewormed, well cared for, ready for prospective owners. Basic health examinations and treatments included in the price, we have pedigree and crossbreed puppies as well as older dogs. Give us a call . . .

Even though this ad sounds reasonable, the dogs are being traded on a large scale as neat package deals. By referring to daily vet care, they want to reassure prospective owners that they are not selling sick animals, but the only vet treatment a healthy puppy really needs is a vaccination! Only very sick animals would need daily vet care.

Irresponsible

2 brindle boxer dogs + 1 gold, with papers, vaccinated, 2 months old, ready to go immediately. Telephone . . .

Allowing people to walk in and buy a dog without a moment's notice is not the action of a responsible breeder.

Secondhand Dog

Irish setter female, 2 years old, no small children, animal shelter.
Telephone . . .

The dog was probably given away to an animal shelter with the comment, "She bit our child." This could have just been an excuse to give away a dog that had become a burden or a nuisance.

Guard Dog

German shepherd, 4½ years old, no children, very good guard dog, Telephone . . .

A guard dog that does not like children would be a very dangerous animal if he ever escaped.

Problem Animal

White Swiss shepherd dog, long hair, 2 years old, anxious, animal shelter.

This is an advertisement for a problem dog. Anxious dogs are slow to trust and may bite out of fear.

How to Spot an Advertisement From a Reputable Breeder:

[. . .] Kennel Club
We are expecting a litter of Kuvasz puppies at the end of October. Would you like to visit the puppies regularly from 2–3 weeks of age? After you have taken your puppy home, we will be in contact to answer all your questions. Visitors always welcome.

This is how an ad from a good breeder should read. It includes proper information for prospective owners and a willingness to be involved after a sale has been made. And although it is not mentioned specifically, it is clear that these puppies will have grown up in close contact with humans.

The Best Puppies

Once you have decided on a breed, then you can begin the search for a reputable breeder. Please remember that the cheapest price is not always the best option. Quality costs more. The proper price means you will not end up paying more later, your puppy will be physically and mentally healthy, and he will have been well cared for in the first few weeks of life.

Families who have no previous experience with dogs are better off choosing a puppy from a reputable and recommended breeder.

Choose With Care

Choose a puppy who has been well looked after by a caring and responsible breeder. Such breeders are not so easy to find, and you may have to wait a while or make a long journey to find the right one. Good things come to those who wait! Also do not be surprised if the breeder is very curious to know all about you.

Caring Breeders Produce Good-Natured Puppies

It is important that your puppy has been able to develop trust in people right from the very beginning and up to his twelfth week of life. If he has been cuddled and played with by people, then he will be well socialized.

Training Makes Your Puppy Smart

Puppies need rules. However, you should let him safely investigate the world around him as much as possible, provide him with the right diet, and make sure he gets plenty of time to play with you.

The mother provides her puppies with nutrition and teaches them self-confidence.

Clean Play Area for Healthy Puppies

Further signs of a reputable breeder are

→ **Cleanliness:** If there is any puppy feces in the cage, these should be fresh feces only and well formed. Diarrhea in puppies is a very bad sign.

→ **Sleeping place:** The puppies should have a warm, dry place to sleep, for example, a cozy corner where they are undisturbed.

→ **Health:** The puppy should have clean fur with no strong odor or bald patches.

→ **Curiosity:** The puppies should be curious and trusting toward the breeder and after gentle coaxing, should come up to see you.

→ **Alertness:** Healthy puppies should be strong, playful, and active. If not on the go, then they will just be relaxing or sleeping. They should not have large, distended bellies, which is a sign of a serious worm infestation.

→ **Appetite:** The puppy should have a good appetite.

→ **Experience of the outdoors:** Exclusively indoor rearing is not ideal. From about the fifth week, puppies should spend at least an hour a day outdoors or they may be fearful of being outside in later life.

Puppies discover the world through play—even if it is only a small world at first.

The Best Environment

The best environment for a puppy offers opportunities for him to solve problems and exercise. He should have different surfaces, such as grass to run through, soil to dig in, and large stones to climb over. A puppy needs tunnels to crawl through and hide in, branches to jump over, and chew toys and balls to fetch and carry.

Which Puppy Would You Like?

A committed breeder will give good advice about which puppy from his or her litter would suit you best. It is a good idea to listen to this advice and take it seriously. You may be drawn to the feistiest puppy in the litter, but if you have no previous experience with dogs, you could quickly become the "underdog."

The mother spends a lot of time and effort training her puppies.

Your Puppy May Still Be With the Breeder,

But the Adventure Has Begun!

When you have chosen your puppy, it will be up to you to ensure he continues to learn about the world and has positive life experiences. His physical appearance is largely defined by his genetics, but his intelligence and character can be molded by you. A good breeder will have given him the best chance in life by developing his physical and mental abilities as far as possible, but ultimately it will be you who shapes his life and ensures he is trusting of people and is a happy dog.

Visit Your Puppy!

When your puppy is around four weeks old and in that all-important formative phase of life, the breeder may invite you to come and visit the puppy.

> *Do not drag out the good-byes—any caring breeder will find it difficult to say good-bye to a puppy, even if that puppy has been very hard work for him or her over the last few weeks. So simply pick your puppy up in your arms and say good-bye!*

> *As long as you are kind to him, your puppy will quickly trust you and think you are the best!*

Getting to Know Each Other

This is not simply generosity on the breeder's part—the breeder will expect you to visit your puppy a few times so that he or she can observe you with the puppy and decide whether you are right for each other. At the same time, you wll have a chance to examine the puppies' living conditions. Take advantage of the regular visits to the puppies to watch how they interact with one another and also with their mother. How far are they allowed to go before the mother intervenes? You can learn a lot just by observing all this. You can also learn how the breeder copes with all the puppies, how he or she carries them, calls them to him or her, fends off their constant playful attacks, and cuddles them.

Responsibilities of the Breeder

Deworming and Vaccination

Responsible breeders will spend as much time as possible with their puppies and will know each one as an individual. The breeder will also ensure the puppies are dewormed from the second week of life; practically every puppy is born with worms or gets worms from the mother's milk, even if the mother has herself been dewormed. In the eighth week of life, the puppies should be vaccinated.

Exploring the outdoors with their mother is a wonderful life lesson that makes puppies very smart . . .

. . . even if it all seems so scary at first.

Puppies are not vaccinated before eight weeks old because they get antibodies from their mother's milk and will not start building their own active immune system until they are weaned. The puppy should not go home with you until at least one week after his first vaccination because it will take a week for his immunity to build up.

Every Puppy Should Have a Vaccination Record

When the breeder gets the puppies vaccinated, they will receive a document with the date of the first vaccination as well as the due date for the second one (at about twelve weeks). Also make sure you know when the puppy was first dewormed so that you do not miss his next deworming medication.

Sales Contract

The breeder will give you a contract that will inform you all about the puppies and the mutual rights and obligations. It may include a health warranty, spay/neuter requirements, what to do if you can no longer care for the dog, and other information.

→ Good Care for Mixed-Breed Dogs

If you buy a mixed-breed puppy, then his litter will lack professional assessment. Therefore, before you take your puppy home, bring someone experienced with you to visit him first. A mixed-breed dog also requires a good upbringing, just as much as any pedigree dog, to ensure he is a sociable dog later in life.

Dog-walking clothes should be practical and easy to clean. When a mischievous puppy jumps up at you, you are bound to get covered in paw prints.

In the first few weeks, set up a good basis for when the puppy gets older. Take time to show him the world and give him plenty of love to gain his trust.

Prepare your home for your new puppy well before you pick him up so that everything is ready, and you can devote all your time to your new "baby." Your puppy will still be very young and need a lot of attention.

Take Your Time

The most important thing in the first few weeks is time. You will soon see that he is worth it. Your puppy is a fascinating creature, and you should make the most of these new experiences. He will bring you a lot of love and fun.

The Formative Weeks

How much time and commitment you invest now will pay off later on. Every experience your puppy has with you over the first few weeks will shape the rest of his life. Spend as much time as you can with your new puppy.

Go Shopping

Get yourself some clothes that are durable. Your puppy will have teeth like needles and equally sharp claws. He will be lively and playful. He will probably be jumping up at you and climbing all over you in all kinds of weather, rain or shine, just to make contact and get reassurance

from you. If you live on the top floor, you will need to carry your puppy up and down the stairs for the first year. You will be amazed how such a small puppy can make such a wet, muddy mess all over your clothes!

Eliminate Any Hazards

Search through your home with a keen eye and ask yourself what could be dangerous for a puppy? And what could get destroyed by him? Puppies are a bit like toddlers—they are incredibly curious and like to investigate their environment by chewing on objects and feeling them with their mouths, and they may even swallow or choke on them. So objects such as paper clips, pens, small toys, pins, brooches, and jewelry could be very dangerous for a puppy.

Put It Away

There will be some things you will need to put out of reach, such as your favorite teddy bear, collectible dolls, cell phone, and anything else that has sentimental

Fence Up the Yard

You will not be able to let your puppy out in the yard without first making sure there is a fence going all the way around. And when he is outside, you will need to supervise him! Get rid of any pesticides, including slug and snail poison. Even organic fertilizers can be dangerous for your puppy if he eats it. Protect your flower beds with fencing or they may be trampled by an overly excited puppy. You also do not want your puppy going to the bathroom in your vegetable garden!

Mine or not? Puppies need to learn which toys they may play with and which objects, such as shoes, although tempting, they must leave alone.

or financial value. A puppy does not know the difference between expensive objects and objects with no value—he will investigate everything!

Baby Gate

To prevent accidents, block up the stairway with a baby gate at the top and the bottom. Stairs with slippery steps can be incredibly dangerous, so if your adult dog eventually goes up and down the stairs, make sure they are covered with a nonslip carpet or rug.

Do not forget to cover or fence in the pond, too. A pond often has steep, slippery edges that could be a deadly trap for a curious puppy.

Leave Home Improvements for Later — Tip

If your house needs improvements, ask your parents or a responsible adult if they can put them off for a while until your puppy has grown up. He is bound to nibble on everything within his reach, so it would be safer to save the house renovations for next year.

Time to Take Your Furry Friend Home
From the First Day On

The first day of a vacation in your household is the best time to pick up your new puppy. If that is not possible, then it is best to pick her up on a Friday afternoon or Saturday morning. This will give your puppy a chance to get to know each family member and have enough time to get used to them before they disappear off to work or school on Monday morning.

After an exhausting first day full of new experiences, your puppy will be content to snuggle up in a blanket that smells like her littermates.

A Cuddle Blanket for Your Puppy

As it gets dark outside, your puppy will soon get tired and may wish she could cuddle up with her brothers and sisters. Ask the breeder for an old blanket with the familiar scent of her littermates on it. When the puppy smells this scent, it should calm her; the smell of her siblings will be a huge comfort to her.

What Did the Breeder Feed Your Puppy?

Find out what food the breeder fed your puppy before you take her home. It is best to give her the same food she is already used to, or if you choose it yourself, make sure it is a puppy food, and follow the feeding instructions. If you want to change the food at any point, do this slowly over a couple of days. Also, when you pick up your puppy from the breeder, do not forget her vaccination records, sales contract, any test reports, and her pedigree papers.

The Drive Home

Bring a pet carrier to transport her in, and make sure it is secure and that she can see you. If it is a long car journey, do not forget to stop for bathroom breaks. Put your puppy on a leash if you take her outside. She may need to urinate in her pet carrier, so make sure you provide her with an old towel to soak up any urine.

New Surroundings

Your little puppy will be incredibly curious about her new home and very eager to explore. If you have a yard, let her explore this first so she can go to the bathroom. If you live in an apartment, you will need to make her a temporary bathroom from a pile of newspapers or you can use housebreaking pads from a pet supply store. If you see her

If you do not want your puppy to lick your face or develop another bad habit, discourage her from doing it right from the beginning.

searching around with her nose to the ground, or squatting, carry her quickly to the newspapers or housebreaking pad and instruct her to urinate by saying something like, "Make pee pee!"

Cozy Bed

Show her all her new toys as well as her bed. A cardboard box with a cozy blanket inside can work. Just make sure it has no staples or any strong chemical smells. Or you can buy a dog bed from a pet supply store. You could also put the blanket with her siblings' scent inside the box. Dogs love to curl up on cozy sheepskin blankets or even just the carpet. Make sure you are there when she wakes up or she might feel lonely.

Familiar Food

Feed her her familiar food at room temperature at the usual times. Call her to eat with her name: "Paddy, come!" She will be curious and come to investigate. She will also connect her name and the invitation "come" with something positive.

This will be useful later when you want to call her to you. After eating, you should encourage her to go to the bathroom.

First Sleep, Then Play

Most puppies will want to keep playing after they have eaten, but this is not a good idea, particularly for large breeds, which are more prone to bloating. So encourage her to have a nap and then she can play afterward.

Ignore her invitation to play if she has just eaten her dinner.

TIPS

Your New Best Friend

Everything Is Strange and New

Your little dog is still just a kid like you, but he has just left his mother and siblings and everything that was familiar to him. Can you imagine how he must be feeling? How would you feel? Lonely and scared? Lost and confused? His new home with you will feel quite strange to him at first. Take extra care in the first few days to treat him with respect and kindness and this will help him feel more at home. Just be there for him, talk to him, play and cuddle, and do not leave him on his own at night. He needs you to make him feel safe and well cared for.

Rowdy and Playful

You will be able to distract him from his sadness quite easily. Just squeeze his favorite squeaky toy or throw his favorite ball. He will soon perk up and become playful, carefree, and bold. The two of you will grow to understand each other very well.

Tug-of-War

All dogs love to play tug-of-war games. They want to test out their strength and see if they can pull the object, such as a knotted rope, out of your hands. There is nothing wrong with a game of tug-of-war, but make sure it does not get out of hand. Although his bite is not exactly painful yet, you do not want him biting your hands. If he nips you, stop playing immediately. This will show him that biting is not allowed!

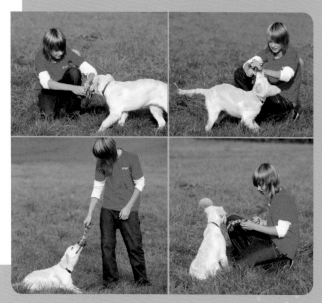

Tricks and Treats

Puppies love to learn new things, and your puppy may enjoy going to obedience school. Feeling useful and learning tricks makes him happy, especially if there are rewards involved. See if you can teach him to give you his paw for a treat!

Rules of Play for Puppies and People

For puppies:

→ Human hands are sensitive. If your puppy bites you, end the game immediately.

→ Always have a toy box at hand with plenty of different toys available. Just think, you would not like it much if your parents kept your toys hidden from you and only let you have them every now and again.

→ Paws down! If your puppy jumps up at you, turn your back on him. Only give him your full attention again when his four paws are firmly on the ground. This is the best way to teach him not to jump up.

For people:

→ If your puppy is sleeping, eating, or going to the bathroom, he does not want to be disturbed. Leave him in peace to do what he needs to do.

→ You are the one who decides when to start or finish a game and how rowdy it gets. If the game gets out of control, then it is best to end it.

→ Puppies have very good ears, so do not make loud noises, such as screaming, when you are close to him. He will respond much better to a soft, kind voice and a delicious treat as a reward.

Dog-Smart in 30 Days

Your puppy will adjust incredibly quickly to his new home. As long as you show him plenty of love, he will adore you and devote himself to you almost immediately. Despite his playfulness and enthusiasm, he is a sensitive little soul. During his first night in his new home, he will need to be with you or he will get anxious.

The First Night

Put his bed next to your bed at night. Remember, if you notice him getting restless, quickly carry him into the yard or to his pile of newspapers or housebreaking pad. If you allow him to, he will happily snuggle up on your bed and feel cozy there.

Your puppy should have as much contact with other dogs as possible, so that he can learn the rules of social etiquette among dogs.

Your dog will feel safer if his bed is next to your bed at night.

Your Puppy Wants to Be With You

If you ban him from the bedroom and make him sleep alone in the kitchen, he will howl all night because as a pack animal, sleeping alone is unnatural for him. He will feel scared. A puppy who is left to his own devices will feel sad. Also, you will not be able to take him out to the yard when he needs to go to the bathroom. He will whine and howl his little heart out if no one is there to comfort him.

Midnight Bathroom Breaks

For the first few nights, you may need to rush outside with him if he needs to go to the bathroom. There will not be much time between your puppy feeling the urge to urinate and actually urinating. He will become restless and get off the bed, if you allow him to sleep there. He is unlikely to urinate on the bed because he will not want to soil his sleeping area.

Nibbling Like There Is No Tomorrow

The puppy will soon feel right at home and gain confidence to go and explore the house out of sheer curiosity. He will use his mouth and his teeth to investigate everything

in sight. Make sure you keep a close eye on him as he wanders around so you can make it clear what is and what is not allowed. Your active little puppy will soon realize that the most common word he will hear is "No!"

Socialization

Your puppy needs regular contact with other dogs as much as possible in order to develop his social skills naturally and to be able to interact safely and harmoniously with other dogs in later life. Unfortunately, encounters with other dogs are not without their risks because not every dog is friendly. Even if your puppy has not had his second vaccination, he should still be socialized with other dogs. If he is kept apart from his own kind out of fears for his health, this could damage his social behavior.

Sniff and Stroll

Your puppy wants to explore the world, so take him outside. Take a dog toy with you, such as a rubber ring, a dog Frisbee®, a piece of material (e.g., denim from an old pair of jeans)—anything he can chew without damaging his teeth or choking. (Small rubber balls are not a good idea.) After a walk or play session in the yard, he will soon be exhausted and fast asleep.

Talk to Him!

If you are home and your puppy is curled up in his bed near you or following you around, this is a great opportunity to have a little conversation. Dogs use the tone of your voice to pick up on your mood. Tell him about the world around him in clear, simple words. Have a chat with him using phrases such as "Let's play a game!" or "Where is your ball?" in an excited tone of voice. If you make it fun and cuddle him and tickle him, he will soon understand more than you realize!

Alternate playing with sleeping. Sometimes he will get so tired, he may fall asleep in the middle of a game!

Contact with other dogs is important. Here, the puppy tests his strength and learns manners.

It may look cute, but looking after a small child and a puppy at the same time is very demanding. Be extra helpful to your parents if you have a little sister or brother and a new puppy!

At a Glance
What Your Puppy Needs

Checklist: Bringing Your Puppy Home

To the breeder's:
- → collar
- → leash
- → towels
- → money
- → address
- → carrier

For the trip home:
- → food from the breeder
- → blanket with littermates' scent
- → vaccination records
- → sales contract
- → receipt
- → any other paperwork

Living Area

Of course, your puppy's living area will be your home, but because puppies are so curious and stick their noses into everything, you should make a few preparations beforehand: block off the stairs, put dangerous or valuable items out of reach or lock them away, and put up a fence in the yard.

Sleeping Area

Your puppy needs her own place to sleep or relax, but it should be in a place where she can see you, for example, a corner of the living room. Give her a basket with a cozy blanket or a pet bed. Let her sleep in the bedroom with you for the first few nights so she does not feel lonely. Keep an eye on her to see if she needs to go to the bathroom. It is up to you and your parents to decide whether or not to let your puppy sleep on your bed, but be aware that once you allow her to do this, she will want to do it forever! Dogs get confused when you suddenly change the rules. You may end up with an upset puppy whining at the side of your bed or outside your bedroom door.

Eating

Your dog will need two sturdy ceramic or stainless-steel bowls, one for food and one for water. Avoid plastic bowls because  they can harbor bacteria in tiny cracks. Make sure she always has access to her water bowl. Feed her the same food as the breeder, at least for the first few weeks.

Walking

When you take your puppy outside, make sure she is wearing a collar with a tag that has her name and your telephone number and that she is on a leash. Check that the collar fits comfortably and is not too tight and that it is adjustable because she will grow very quickly! Choose either leather or nylon. A leash between 5 and 6.5 feet long and adjustable in length is best. It is known as a retractable leash. You can lengthen the leash when you want to give your puppy more freedom and shorten it when you want to keep her close to you.

Playing

You can find a variety of puppy toys in pet supply stores and many regular stores. These toys include balls, knotted ropes, squeaky toys, Frisbees®, and rubber chew toys. Choose toys you think she will enjoy playing with and make sure they are safe for her. You could also make her some toys, for example, with rope.

Grooming

Depending on the breed, you may need to groom your puppy regularly. For short-haired breeds, grooming her once a week with a soft brush will be enough, but for long-haired breeds, you will need to buy a special comb. Your breeder will be happy to advise you what type of comb to buy. Also ask the breeder or your veterinarian about trimming your puppy's claws and brushing her teeth!

Health Insurance?

Puppies are naturally lively and accidents may happen. Some companies offer pet health insurance to help pay vet bills in case your dog gets sick or hurt. Ask your parents to do some research so they can decide if it would be worth getting.

Feeding and Caring for Your Puppy

What Puppies Want to Eat
A Delicious, Healthy Diet

If it were up to your puppy, he would happily munch on some deer droppings, a baby mouse, some rose hips, and a few blades of grass. But with all the dangerous chemicals we have in our environment, he could quite easily eat something poisonous. Also, just the thought of your puppy eating any kind of feces and then trying to lick your face may be enough to make you gag! But when we say deer waste, it is not the same stuff you may find lying in the grass. Read on to learn more.

Feed Him What He Knows

Puppies do not know what is good for them and what is bad for them. So it is up to us to decide what our little four-legged friends should eat. Nevertheless, there is no harm in the odd, healthy treat. Take the advice of the breeder to heart and feed your puppy whichever food he is used to eating. If you want to feed your puppy a different kind of food, change it gradually over a few days. Ask your vet what type of food is best for your pet.

Make sure your puppy always has access to a large bowl of fresh water. Fill it up several times a day, especially if the weather is warm. If you feed your puppy dry food, he will need to drink more water.

This puppy cannot help dipping his long ears into his food bowl!

Several Meals a Day

Feed your puppy four times a day for the first few weeks. Then, reduce it to three times a day, and by the time he is between nine and twelve months of age, he should be on two meals a day. If possible, feed him at the same times every day and give him food that is room temperature, not food that has come straight out of the refrigerator. If your puppy is a large breed, put his food on a small table so he does not strain his back reaching down to eat it. Do not leave leftover wet food in the bowl because it will spoil very quickly. However, if you feed him dry food, you can leave this out in his bowl for him to eat whenever he wants.

Deer Droppings for Breakfast

Like his ancestor the wolf, a dog is a carnivore, or meat eater, but not exclusively. When a predator eats a prey animal, everything is digested, including bone, cartilage, skin, feathers, and the stomach contents of the prey. The herbivores among the prey animals, such as deer, mice, rabbits, hares, and partridges, are all vegetarian and can digest more or less everything they eat. They need a lot of bacteria to break down this food. Predigested plant foods are an important part of a dog's diet.

Yummy Veggies

Give your dog a variety of plant foods. They should be prepared in a certain way so your dog can digest them (chop them up, cook them, and add oil).

A rawhide chew will keep your dog busy for hours!

Dog Chews

In addition to his main food, your dog will need to chew on rawhide, or dog chews and the like. At about the age of four months, he will lose his baby teeth and feel a strong urge to chew as his adult teeth grow in. Real bones can be dangerous, especially if they are cooked, because they become brittle and can splinter, which could lead to injuries and blockages in his stomach. Chicken bones are a bad idea. Your puppy could choke on them.

→ What a Puppy Is Not Allowed to Eat

Onions, grapes, and chocolate are just a few examples of human foods that are toxic to dogs. A bar of chocolate contains a chemical called theobromine in the cocoa powder, which can be deadly for a dog. So pay attention to what your dog eats.

Picking the Right Food

Navigating the Jungle of Food Choices

Your dog may not be a fussy eater, but make sure his food is of good quality. Like us, our dogs live in an age of fast-food convenience. Just open a can and spoon out the meal into the serving bowl. Also, a few handfuls of dry food will ensure he receives the right nutrition, provided it is of good quality. The cheapest dog foods do not use the best ingredients. But be careful—the most expensive dog foods are not always the best ones either!

There are many different types of dog food available on the market. Choose carefully and pay attention to ingredients. Your breeder or your vet will also be able to advise you on what is best.

Your dog depends on you to make the right food choices for him!

Food Quality

A reputable dog food manufacturer will ensure that all the vital ingredients keep the dog fit and healthy. You should also choose a food that your dog can tolerate well.

Read the Labels

Read the labels carefully. It is also a good idea to get advice from the vet or the breeder. Then, once you have made a short list of different types of food, you could also ask the manufacturer to answer any questions you may have. Some companies have a customer service number you can call. In most breeds, after about seven months, the majority of the growth spurts are finished and the animal will reach puberty by this time. Therefore, good nutrition for the first few months of a puppy's life is vital.

Less Is More

Perhaps you assumed that a big dog will eat a lot and a small dog not very much? This may be true in some cases. But a gentle giant of a dog that is slow to move and really rather lazy will need less food than an athletic, medium-sized dog, so body weight is not the only guideline. For example, a border collie who does agility classes requires more food than a chilled-out Bernese mountain dog.

Special Diets for Large Breeds

The larger your puppy, the more serious the consequences of malnutrition. On the other hand, you will need to ensure you are not giving him too much food because he may grow too fast or become overweight, which will have a negative impact on his joints. Go for quality over quantity—less is more. You can buy dog food aimed especially at certain types of breeds.

Daily Food Intake

It is not only the size of your dog, but also the temperament and his living conditions which affect his daily food requirement. Just as with humans, some dogs do tend to overeat. Detailed information concerning exact quantities is therefore not possible, so follow the advice of the breeder, take into account the information on the packaging, and also keep an eye on your dog. For example, if he appears too thin or constantly hungry then feed him a bit more.

Medium and Small Breeds

Your puppy should eat until he is satisfied, but do not let him overeat. It is a mistake to believe that a chubby puppy will grow into a sturdy adult dog. Instead, he is more likely to become just a fat adult dog with all the health problems that come with being overweight.

A puppy will need the right food to help him develop into a healthy adult dog.

All in One

If you choose to feed your dog a "complete food," which contains all the vitamins and minerals he needs, then do not give him any extra vitamins or minerals. An excess of minerals, for example, can build up in the joints of young dogs. You could feed him a varied diet by adding such things as apple, parsley, steamed carrots, a spoonful of porridge or soft brown rice, cottage cheese or something similar, but do not make it too rich in protein.

Puppy Food for the First Time

There are different specially prepared foods for every age and every level of activity (as well as a special diet for dogs that suffer from certain illnesses). Use only puppy food for your puppy and then adult food when he grows up.

What Is in It? What Is It Made Of? What Should You Look Out For?

Animal by-products include fur, hooves, bone, etc.

Antioxidants are synthetic, or man-made, and prevent the fat in dry food from going rancid.

Ash is the remaining minerals after a food has been burned to 1112°F.

Calcium-phosphorus ratio is the balance of calcium and phosphorus. An ideal ratio is 1.2 to 1 (calcium to phosphate).

Chondroitin is an important substance from shark cartilage added to dog food to protect the joints.

A complete food contains all the essential nutrients in the correct amounts. You do not need to add anything else!

Crude fiber is indigestible fiber.

Disodium glutamate (and other glutamates) is an unnecessary flavor enhancer.

Dry food is also known as kibble. A puppy needs much less dry food than wet food to get the required amount of energy. This is because wet food contains a lot of water.

Dyes in dog food are unnecessary. Your dog does not care how pretty his food looks. What really matters is its taste and nutritional value! Some dogs may even be allergic to certain food dyes.

Emulsifiers ensure that fat and water components combine properly and are harmless.

Expiration date is important because vitamins break down quite quickly.

Flavoring agents are added to make the food smell good, and are usually artificially manufactured and totally unnecessary.

Food additives are chemicals added to food, such as preservatives, artificial dyes, emulsifiers, and antioxidants approved by the U.S. Food and Drug Administration. However, the body does not need these and they can often cause allergies. For a list of additives and more information, visit the U.S. Food and Drug Administration Web site. Additives are present in all prepared food. Generally the less artificial substances there are, the better.

Food supplements should not be fed alone to the dog. For example, flakes of corn, which provide extra vitamins and minerals, can be added to the meat.

Glucosamine is key for growth. Amino sugars support bone and cartilage growth and can help prevent hip and elbow dysplasia.

Identical to nature is a phrase used to describe a synthetic additive.

Kilocalories give the energy content of the food.

Lysine and methionine are amino acids. The higher the content of natural lysine and methionine in the meat, the better the quality.

Meat and bone meal is a low-cost meat used in dog food.

Meaty chunks are chopped-up meat mixed with grains.

Minerals include potassium, sodium, calcium, magnesium, phosphorus (phosphate), and chlorine (chloride).

Organic dog food contains no artificial substances. The ingredients include plant material not treated with pesticides or synthetic fertilizers and meat from animals not treated with antibiotics or growth hormones.

Puppy food is very rich in nutrients and high in calories. You should switch to adult food once your dog begins to reach maturity, which can be anywhere from seven months to two years of age, depending on the breed. Small dogs mature faster than large dogs.

Quality is often, but not always, indicated by price. A good quality food could cost a lot more than a bad quality food. But expensive food is not always high quality!

Soy is a vegetable protein. It can trigger allergies.

Supplemental feeding means the food should be fed in combination with other types of food. It is not a complete food.

Trace elements include iron, zinc, fluorine (fluoride), sulfur (sulfate), iodine, cobalt, copper, manganese, and selenium. They are often combined with vitamins and minerals and added to the food.

Vitamin supplements can be useful because vitamins are lost when food is heated.

Water content in dry food is much lower (7 to 9 percent) than in wet food. For wet food, it is up to 80 percent.

Fresh Food
Home-Cooked Meals

A Halloween toy that is great to play with . . . and edible, too!

Ask your vet if it is a good idea to prepare one meal a day for your puppy, and then feed him wet or dry food for the remaining meals. Always ask your parents for help when preparing the meal. Remember that quality is more important than quantity. The ratio of meat (protein) to other foods (carbohydrates, dietary fiber) should be about two-thirds to one-third. So first, put the cooked, unseasoned meat in the bowl, and then use half that amount of vegetables and other foods. Add some cooled water that was used to cook the vegetables, mix it up, and serve it at room temperature.

Mixing Foods

Good foods to mix in with the meat are cooked brown rice, noodles, porridge, cooked carrots and potatoes, grated apple, mashed banana, and parsley. You should avoid feeding your puppy table scraps. Although carrots and whole wheat pasta without any seasoning or sauces will not hurt your pet, anything very fatty, sugary, or spicy is a bad idea.

Slow-Growing

If your puppy grows very rapidly, please be extra careful about what you feed him. Puppies and young dogs of larger and also some smaller breeds need to grow slowly in order to avoid joint problems. Make sure the protein value in their food is not more than 25 percent and the fat content is less than 15 percent.

→ 10 Tips for Preparing Food Yourself

1. Ask your vet if it is okay to feed homemade food to your puppy, what kinds of food to include, and how much of each ingredient. Ask a responsible adult to help you.

2. Lamb, beef, venison, chicken, and fish are ideal. Avoid pork products. Do not feed your dog raw or undercooked pork.

3. Fatty, sugary, and spicy foods should not be given to dogs.

4. Raw meat, although easily digestible for a dog, can be contaminated with disease-causing bacteria.

5. Do not feed your dog spoiled food.

6. Avoid using offal (leftover meats from a butchered animal) such as liver and kidney because these contain toxins.

7. Cooked meat should be salted sparingly with iodized salt. Raw meat does not need salt.

8. A few drops of sunflower oil (up to a tablespoon, depending on the size of the puppy) will make food more digestible.

9. Acidified milk products, such as yogurt and cottage cheese, contain healthy protein, calcium, and many important bacteria that keep your dog's digestive tract working well.

10. Add mineral food supplements specifically for puppies according to the manufacturer's instructions. Do not use any more than is specified!

There are several advantages to feeding your dog home-cooked food: it is fresh; it contains natural ingredients and vitamins; it is a wholesome way to eat; and, last but not least, it provides digestive bacteria.

Fulfill Your Dog's Dreams
Food for the Soul

Spoil your puppy rotten! Give her lots of cuddles, go on adventures together, and do not leave her on her own.

"Spoil your dog rotten!" Some people will say you should not do this, but why not? Just make sure you spoil your dog in the right way so that she leads the best life possible.

Pamper Her

The best way to pamper her is in ways that contribute to her well-being. An extra portion of food is not the way to do this. An extra cuddle or walk are the best ways to treat her and make her happy. An anxious dog needs affection and reassurance, not excess food. Not being able to say "no" to your puppy does not make her life better. An overfed, undisciplined dog who barks constantly is no one's idea of an ideal pet.

Go to Her

Good care begins when you consider her and are concerned for her, which is just what your puppy needs. Spend time with her when she needs you most. Find the correct mix of adventure, play, sleep, walks, and cuddles. Talk to her, make her feel safe, and do not leave her on her own if you can help it. In turn, she will thank you for being such a loyal friend.

This puppy is still a little afraid. Luckily her owner is on hand to reassure her.

Cozy Sleeping Space

A puppy will spend half the day asleep—but is it good sleep? From a puppy's point of view, the best sleeping place was with her mother and littermates where she felt cozy, warm, and safe. Now suddenly, she has to sleep in a bed all by herself in a different room from her new parent. She will not like that, so make sure you are always nearby, at least while she is still a baby and getting used to her new surroundings.

Safe at Your Side

Your puppy will want you nearby as often as possible. Put her bed in a cozy place in the room where you spend most of your time. She will not want to be alone. In any case, your puppy will want to be by your side when you finally have time to relax in the evening. If she decides to set up camp under the coffee table, let her. She will find her own places to sleep in.

Give Her a Bed

You can find dog beds at many pet supply stores. Or you can get creative and make one yourself by placing a cushion inside a basket. If you decide to buy her a basket, get one made from natural materials, if possible. Make sure it is not painted or treated with chemicals. A glossy finish may look nice but that is because it has been treated with all sorts of chemicals! Also make sure her basket is not easy to chew and destroy. You can line the basket with an old blanket. A new dog cushion should be washed before use. A nice, soft cushion inside your dog's basket makes it cozy and inviting.

What Your Puppy Loves

→ **Friendly chatter.** Talking to your dog makes her happy, even if she cannot understand what you are saying. Chat with her whenever you can, and use her name often. Always use the same words for the same things, and then she will soon understand which objects you are talking about, for example, "Time for walkies!" She will soon learn what this means and jump up in excitement when she hears you say these magic words!

→ **Doing activities together.** Classes such as agility, obedience, scent-tracking, or doggy yoga will be great for both of you.

→ **Exploring the world with you.** Take a walk with your puppy. At first, do not go too far, just around the block and out in the yard. And then, as she gets older, you can take her on longer walks and hikes.

Chewing Her Bed   **Tip**

If your puppy has managed to chew bits and pieces from her bed, these could be dangerous and cause her to choke. If she still continues to chew her bed despite your attempts to stop her, you may need to get rid of the bed and buy a simple dog cushion or even just a blanket.

→ **Being with you at night.** Being alone makes a puppy feel anxious. All she wants is to be with you. Put her bed next to yours so she can sleep soundly and feel safe all night.

→ **Living in harmony.** Consider her needs and if you follow all the points above, you can have a blissfully happy pet and loyal companion.

Game on! It is not just dogs who learn through play. Whether old or young, human beings learn through play as well.

A Small Sting With a Big Impact

Some dogs love their veterinarian and bound joyfully into the office and enjoy having a curious sniff of everything around them. They do not have the slightest anxiety about being there, despite the fact the waiting room may have plenty of anxious dogs trembling next to their owners.

Picking Up on Your Vibes

The skill of the veterinarian is not the only thing that determines whether your dog is happy to go to the vet's office or becomes very anxious. Her own individual character as well as any fear she may sense from you play big parts. Dogs can pick up on our fears and anxieties. Vaccinations are nothing to worry about, so stay calm and relaxed for your dog.

Which Veterinarian?

A vaccination involves a small prick in the skin from a needle attached to a syringe. If the vet is really good, the dog will barely feel it and the vet should distract the dog afterward by stroking her or playing with her so that she forgets about what just happened. Choose a practice with a vet who is experienced, shows empathy and understanding, and interacts well with your dog. You could ask other dog owners you know which vets they visit.

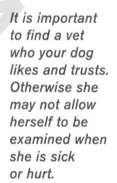

It is important to find a vet who your dog likes and trusts. Otherwise she may not allow herself to be examined when she is sick or hurt.

Fuss-Free Vaccinations

→ Do not forget to take your puppy's vaccination record with you to the vet's office and make sure she is on a leash.

→ Allow your dog to have contact with other dogs in the waiting room as long as they are friendly and not contagious in any way. If you are unsure, then keep your puppy on your lap.

→ Do not let your puppy drink water left out in the waiting room because a sick dog might have drunk from it.

→ Find out when your dog needs deworming treatment and buy the medicine while you are there.

→ Also get some flea and tick control medicine at the same time.

→ Ask for the telephone number of the closest emergency veterinary clinic that is open on weekends and at night when the regular vet's office is closed.

→ A few days after the vaccination, take it easy with your puppy, and give her plenty of time to relax as her body will be making antibodies and building up immunity.

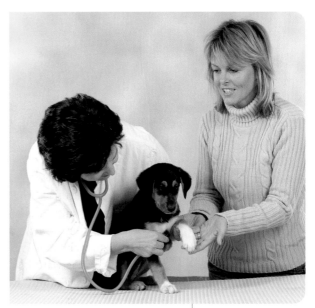

Time for the Next Vaccination

When the puppy is twelve weeks old, about two to four weeks after you bring her home from the breeder, she will need her second vaccination. It is up to you to remember when this is and book an appointment at the right time.

Required Vaccinations

All puppies must be vaccinated against distemper, hepatitis, rabies, and parvovirus. Your veterinarian may recommend other vaccinations, such as leptospirosis, coronavirus, parainfluenza, kennel cough, or Lyme disease, depending on your dog's age, breed, health, and how likely she is to contract the disease. There may be additional vaccines if you are going to take her to a dog show or travel abroad with her. Once she has had her second injection, her vaccinations are complete, and she will need annual boosters from then on. Also, do not forget her tick, flea, and heartworm medication. You can get this when you go to the vet's office.

A Checkup for Reassurance

The vet will check your puppy's paws, fur, skin, and ears. If your puppy is male, the vet will check to see if the testicles have descended, meaning they are in the scrotum and not still inside the body. Do not worry if they have not yet descended. However, after the age of eight months, if the testicles are still inside the abdomen, then your dog will need an operation to remove them, otherwise they may form cancerous cells. Here is a sample vaccination schedule. Remember that your dog's vaccinations may be different.

Your dog will decide for herself whether she thinks a trip to the vet is scary or not.

→ Vaccines

Age	Vaccination
6–8 weeks	parvovirus, kennel cough
8–10 weeks	distemper, hepatitis (HCC), leptospirosis
10–12 weeks	parvovirus, kennel cough
12–14 weeks	distemper, hepatitis (HCC), rabies
16 weeks	parvovirus
Annual boosters	leptospirosis, parvovirus, distemper, hepatitis (HCC), kennel cough, rabies

Is Your Dog Sick?
Signs of Illness

A puppy has the best chance in life when he comes from healthy parents, is brought up in an environment appropriate to his breed, and does not leave his mother before he is eight weeks.

Some Puppies Are Ill From Day One

The health of a puppy who has been rescued from the streets, sold at a pet shop, or bought from a dog trader could be another matter. Often these puppies are sold at the age of four to six weeks and are very sickly. It is likely they have not been vaccinated either.

Go Through the Checklist

Look at the checklist on page 47. If your puppy is showing any of these signs then you should take him to the vet immediately. Puppies that are ill can die within a very short period of time so do not delay. Have the address and number to an emergency veterinary clinic handy.

Joint Problems

Depending on the breed, many young dogs have serious joint problems and can soon become lame. German shepherds, golden retrievers, Labrador retrievers, dachshunds, and Saint Bernards are among the breeds that are prone to joint disorders such as arthritis. You can help prevent these sorts of problems in some cases, for example, do not let him play on slippery floors or walk him too far when he is little. Unfortunately some disorders are genetic, such as hip dysplasia, and he may need an operation to replace a hip or knee joint. Puppies can sometimes have problems with their joints while they are still growing, so see your vet if you notice your dog is limping.

Pimples on the Belly

Puppies have very sensitive bellies, and sometimes the skin can become covered in small pimples. Sometimes an ointment or cream can help get rid of these.

Write down any questions you want to ask before you go to the vet's office, or you may forget what you wanted to ask.

Rough games could cause injuries, and long walks or running with you could be harmful to your puppy's joints when he is still growing.

Gastrointestinal Disorders

Gastrointestinal problems are not unusual. If your puppy is in good health but vomits his food or has diarrhea every once in a while, there is no need to panic. This could happen because he has eaten something that does not agree with him. If it reoccurs then think about what could be causing it. A common cause of gastrointestinal problems is intolerance to a certain food. Did you feed him a piece of spicy sausage, for example? Some dogs have food allergies and have bad reactions to certain ingredients.

Symptoms of Poisoning

If you suspect your puppy is suffering from poisoning (from medicine, detergents, insecticides, fertilizers, etc.), then contact your vet immediately! You could save your puppy's life if you are able to tell the vet what you think he may have eaten. For example, take the aspirin packet or bottle of detergent with you. If you do not know what has caused it, then take a sample of his vomit with you.

Signs of Illness

→ **fatigue, lack of playfulness**
→ **loss of appetite**
→ **watery or red eyes**
→ **diarrhea, possibly bloody**
→ **vomiting repeatedly**
→ **dull coat with bare patches and dry skin**
→ **bloated, distended abdomen (sign of worms)**
→ **cough that sounds as if something is stuck in the throat**
→ **mucus in the nose**
→ **brownish, dirty ear passages (mites!)**

Has your little whirlwind suddenly lost his appetite and become listless and run down? Then it is time to take him to the vet.

Observe His Behavior

If you notice anything different about your puppy's behavior, for example, fatigue, apathy, restlessness, hunched posture, and whining, then take him to the vet.

You Are Your Puppy's Voice

At the vet, you are the voice of your puppy. Your dog's health depends on your good observation skills and your accurate description to the vet. If the vet is given the wrong information or insufficient information, this may result in your puppy receiving the wrong treatment.

Ticks, Fleas, and Other Pests

When you take your dog home with you for the first time, he may not be the only new creature in the house! Fleas or ticks can make him feel unwell, as can lice, mites, and other pests. Once parasites have taken hold, they can create a lot of havoc. However, infestations can be avoided.

Zap Those Fleas

First, it is over there . . . . Now, it is here . . . . All of a sudden, it is gone! It is quite easy to spot a flea—a flea jumps! And it is very difficult to catch because by the time you have blinked, it will have jumped again. The best chance of catching a flea is when it is crawling out of the dog's fur. Use a pincer grip with your index finger and thumb to remove it from the fur. Fleas are very difficult to crush. If you have done this before, you will know to listen out for the popping sound when you have crushed them successfully. If not, then it is best to drown them in a glass of water.

Combat the Flea Infestation

If you find black dirt on your dog's skin, place it on a paper towel and press it into the paper. If you see a reddish color, then it is flea dirt with undigested blood residue. Fleas drink more blood than they can digest.

Constant scratching and bald patches in the fur indicate a mite, fungus, or flea infestation. It could also be a sign of an allergy, so get your vet to take a look.

If you suspect a flea infestation, then repeatedly comb your dog's fur with a flea comb (you can buy one from any pet supply shop). There are also flea-killing sprays and shampoos available. It is flea season all year around because the flea offspring hatch from eggs in warm, hidden places in your house or shed. You can get rid of flea eggs by thoroughly vacuuming the nooks and crannies in your house.

From Dog to Dog

Fleas can jump from dog to dog. Fleas can also transfer tapeworm to your dog, so you will need to give him regular deworming medicine to kill these off, too. Also check for worms in his feces.

Getting Rid of Ticks

That shimmering blue or beige pea-sized wart that has suddenly appeared on your puppy is most likely a tick! Ticks are most active in warm weather, but they are around in the winter, too, as long as the

Do Not Rub It With Olive Oil

Forget what you may have read about dabbing a tick with olive oil or similar substances. If you do this, it will trigger an alarm response in the tick and it will spit toxins into the bite wound. Because

Although fleas can jump from dog to dog, not all scratching is a sign of a flea infestation. It could be that the dog's collar is annoying him and making him itch.

temperature is not freezing. Hungry ticks lurk on bushes and high grass and fall onto chosen victims when they brush by. You can buy a special tick remover from any pet supply shop, which is quite easy to use once you have the hang of it.

Ticks in Sensitive Places

Ticks in problem areas such as eyelids, genitals, in the ear, or on the mouth can be very difficult to remove. Leave them a few hours so they have drunk enough blood to grow to a larger size, then they will be easier to remove. When they get full, ticks fall off by themselves anyway. It may be best to just leave them be because if they are not removed properly, the mouthparts may stay in the skin, which can lead to inflammation.

they transmit meningitis and Lyme disease, you should avoid provoking this reaction. It is possible to get a vaccination for Lyme disease but not all vets agree on whether this is actually effective or not.

Heartworm Prevention

Heartworm disease is caused by parasites that live in the arteries, lungs, and hearts of dogs, and it is spread through bites from infected mosquitoes. It is a serious disease that can be fatal. There are several ways to prevent heartworm disease in your puppy. You can give him daily and monthly tablets or chewables, monthly topicals, or six-month injections.

Tip

No Flea Collars!

Do not harm your puppy with a flea collar. These collars come with warnings stating they are poisonous to children. And if they are poisonous to children, then they will definitely be poisonous to your puppy, too!

Grooming Your Puppy

Get your puppy used to being groomed and cared for as early on as possible so that he will not protest as much later in life. If you accidentally hurt him, he will be frightened and struggle, and from then on be scared of any grooming you may need to do.

Baby Fur

Puppies have short, teddy-bear-like baby fur, and as long as he lives in a clean house, you will barely need to groom him. You could stroke him with a rubber-studded grooming mitt, which will brush him and also give him a nice massage at the same time. If he has something stuck in his fur, use a damp cloth to remove it and then towel dry him gently but thoroughly. For puppies that will later grow very dense or long coats, getting him used to grooming is a must!

Off to the Hairdresser

Whether a dog needs a professional dog groomer really depends on the breed. A poodle, for example, will need regular grooming. Any other breed that needs intensive grooming should get used to this experience from a young age. He will be very unsure of strange people grooming him at first!

Puppies Do Not Need Baths!

Do not bathe him unless you absolutely have to. If he has a bath, chances are he will get cold and possibly sick. Save baths for emergencies only.

Keep the Head Dry

If he jumps into a muddy puddle or has rolled around in waste, then he will need a bath. Fill the bath up with warm water up to his tummy, and use a pitcher to gently pour water all over his back. Keep his head dry unless it is completely caked in filth. Otherwise, you can just use a damp cloth to clean his face. Accidentally getting water in your puppy's ears can lead to an infection. Use a bit of puppy shampoo and lather it up in his fur. Do not use shampoo made for people. The chemicals could irritate your puppy's skin. Talk to him soothingly as you wash him—he probably will not enjoy this experience so be gentle and kind to him. Do not use force in any way. Rinse his coat thoroughly and stand back while he shakes himself off! Dry him off completely with a towel and then play with him for a bit so he does not sit and shiver. Do not let him go outside on cold days until he is completely dry.

A little dirt from the yard is not enough to justify a bath. Simply clean his legs and stomach with an old damp cloth.

Step-by-Step Puppy Care

Even if your young dog has professional grooming appointments, you can also groom him and give him a quick health check at the same time!

Ears

Do not clean out his ears with cotton swabs. This could be painful for him and the canine ear is self-cleaning anyway. If his ears are very mucky, this could be a sign of a mite infestation, so take him to the vet.

Short Claws and Clean Paws

Sharp puppy claws will gradually wear down and become blunt. You may need to clip the dewclaws on the front paws. If you find clipping difficult, you could try filing them, or get the vet to clip his claws if you are not sure how to do it. In the winter, wash the road salt off his paws to stop him from licking it off himself.

Teeth

The puppy cleans his teeth by gnawing on dog chews. As he grows, check that all his baby teeth have fallen out and that his adult teeth are not growing over them. See a vet if you think something is not right.

Eyes

Healthy eyes should not be constantly watery. If your puppy always has watery eyes, then take him to the vet. It could be caused by ingrown eyelashes or perhaps an allergy. Wipe his eyes carefully every morning to prevent the buildup of crust.

Use a damp cloth to gently wipe crust from his eyes.

Check the ears for gunk. This is particularly important for dogs with large, floppy ears.

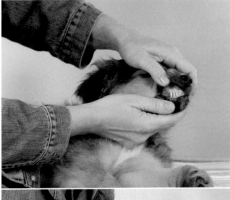

When the adult teeth come through, check that all the baby teeth have fallen out.

Check the paws. Limping is a sure sign something is wrong. Are his claws too long?

My Care Plan

Nutrition Overview

For the first few days, feed your puppy with the same food the breeder gave him.

→ **Later On**

Feed him puppy food up to the age of seven months to a year, but this does not apply to large breeds, as the bigger the dog, the slower he should grow. Use a special type of food aimed at young dogs until he is a year old.

A Mixture of Meals: If you want to prepare your puppy's food yourself, check with your vet first. You may make your dog one meal per day and then use wet or dry food for the other meals. The home-cooked meal should be two-thirds meat and one-third carbohydrates (cereals, bread, potatoes, pasta, rice), or try cottage cheese or yogurt.

Number of Meals: Feed him four times daily at first, then gradually reduce it to twice a day when the dog is a year old. Encourage him to have a nap after eating.

Daily

Food and Water

Clean out the food and water bowls. Your dog should always have fresh water available.

Walks

In the first year, walks should be quite short because the puppy's joints cannot take too much stress while they are still growing. However, he will need the toilet more often when he is little, so let him out as often as possible to do his business.

Training

Start training him right away; he will learn more quickly when he is young. Keep training sessions short and fun. Teach him one thing at a time, such as "sit" or "stay" or "come." Training this way is fun for your puppy and will strengthen the canine-human bond between the two of you.

Cuddling and Playing

Spend as much time cuddling him and playing with him as possible. Explore the world together and enjoy your adventures.

Coat Care

Long-haired breeds should be brushed daily, but short-haired dogs only need to be groomed once a week. Wipe the crust or gunk from his eyes in the mornings, and check him for ticks all year around.

Weekly

Health Check

Are the ears clean? The claws neat? The eyes shiny? Examine your puppy carefully. Look in his mouth as well. Make sure you are gentle with him. He may wriggle at first, but he will soon get used to this attention. Do not forget to brush his coat, too.

Clean His Bed

Wash his bed and blankets about once a week.

Off to Doggy School

Make the most of his first few weeks by taking him to puppy school, if you can. This is the perfect way for him to make social contact with other puppies, getting to know them and having a great time playing with them. Also take him out in the fresh air and get him used to being outside.

Monthly

Combat Pests

Give him monthly flea and tick treatments, especially in the summer, and also deworm him regularly. Your vet will explain how often you should do this. Also, do not forget his annual vaccinations.

Dog Groomer

Some breeds have to be trimmed regularly. This will need to be done every six to eight weeks. It is a good idea to take your short-haired dog to the occasional grooming appointment, just so that he becomes familiar with the process.

Accessories Check

Check his collar and leash for any damage. Wash it if necessary. Also check all his toys and throw away or replace any toys that are damaged.

Training Your Puppy

Rules of the Pack

Lessons Learned Early in Life

Before your puppy came to you, she already had important experiences, which will have shaped her life in a certain way. She learned how to feed from her mother, enjoyed her warmth and affection, and realized that sometimes she was patient and playful yet also determined to train her. Your dog will have been reprimanded at some point by her mother during play.

University of Life

Your puppy is a keen observer. She will soon pick up on what makes you fearful, happy, or excited.

Although the actual formative phase is over, young dogs can still learn a lot from their life experiences. You can use this time to get your puppy used to all the important situations she is likely to come across in her lifetime. So in the beginning, explore the world with her and get her used to things such as traffic, buses, other pets, or the mail carrier. She needs these experiences so make sure she gets plenty of them!

Learning Valuable Lessons as Part of a Pack

Even as a very little puppy, she will have learned that life is not always easy, and she cannot always get her own way. She may have tried to muscle in on her siblings' feeding time and been rebuffed by her mother. She will also have found that her siblings were great playmates and great to snuggle up with, but she is bound to have got into a few fights with them and been reprimanded for tugging too hard on their ears or tails. Although your puppy may well have won a few of these fights, she also will have learned that she cannot win and be the strongest every time. A puppy soon learns to accept her limitations and know her place in the pack. A hierarchy is quickly formed, which then makes it possible to live peacefully with others.

Where Does the Human Playmate Fit Into All This?

Your puppy's interactions with her mother and littermates are not the only relationships she learned from early in life. As her first experience with a human, your puppy's contact with the breeder also influenced how your puppy views the world. She learned to recognize the smell of a human and linked this with a friendly voice and caressing hands. She also will have learned that while tugging on people's socks, for example, a cry of "ouch!" meant that humans are vulnerable, too, and must be treated with care, just like her mother and siblings.

New Puppy Parent

Gradually the puppy learns that this human playmate brings her tasty things to eat! So it is no wonder that a puppy shows fascination with people by about the age of six to eight weeks. She will not be too sad to leave her mother or her brothers and sisters. She will form a new pack with you and your family!

Your Puppy Needs to Be Trained

Behavioral problems can develop if the young dog does not have the appropriate training from someone with leadership qualities. The puppy needs to learn right from the start that you are the one in charge, the alpha dog in her new pack. You decide how long to play with her, you provide the food, and if she does not behave then she does not get any treats. You decide

on her sleeping place, where to take her every day, and when to leave her at home. And what she gets in return is a loving owner who gives her lots of cuddles and attention. She will soon realize that humans are very special creatures; we have hands that can stroke and soothe and we can make her feel safe and loved.

Offer your puppy something tasty and she will soon come running.

The First Trip Outdoors

For a puppy, long walks are too demanding and harmful to her joints. However, she still needs stimulation. She will want to explore her environment and make contact with other dogs. Put her on a leash and take her out on a sniff-and-stroll outing around the neighborhood. Depending on her confidence level, you can take her just a few feet from the front door or walk her around the block.

Heel

Between the ages of eight to sixteen weeks, she will feel a strong desire to walk very close to you for protection. Practice calling her by taking her to a safe enclosed area, and when she is a few feet away from you, call her name. When she runs toward you, reward and praise her.

When she is outside, give your puppy time to sniff and safely investigate cars, baby carriages, bikes, birds, falling leaves—it is all new and fascinating to her.

How the Puppy Protects Herself

Pretty soon, you will come across another dog during your walk. You may worry that your puppy could get bitten, but try not to be too anxious. Most dogs are used to puppies, and your puppy will instinctively employ submissive body language if she is fearful. She may throw herself on her back and expose her tummy, whine, or urinate if she is frightened. If properly socialized, the other dog should pick up on this and leave her alone. But do keep a close watch while they interact.

On a Leash

Hopefully your puppy will get along just fine with other dogs she encounters on her walks. However, just to be on the safe side, keep her close to you or pick her up when you see another dog coming toward you. If you are in an off-leash area in a dog park, put her on a leash until you are sure it is safe. Check with the owner whether it is okay to let both dogs greet and play with each other. Unfortunately, there are many owners whose dogs do not socialize with other dogs. Those dogs or even the owners themselves may be afraid or disapproving of other dogs who run up to them.

Learning Social Behavior

Puppies need to have plenty of contact with other dogs. In these first few weeks, they learn skills for life, and if your dog has not learned something by then, she may learn it with difficulty later on or not at all. She may not be able to learn how to tolerate other dogs, how to play safely, and how to keep the peace among her doggy friends. However, you should be careful about taking your puppy to someone else's house if he or she has an adult dog living there. Female dogs in particular can be aggressive and may bite, and although males are slightly more tolerant, you should still be careful.

This little springer spaniel has found something that interests her. Give your puppy time to observe and investigate everything around her, but keep a close eye on her.

→ Playtime for Puppies

Ask a responsible adult for permission before you start looking for a dog walking club, a dog sports clubs, or dog school. If it is okay, then you could ask your breeder or search the Internet for dog-related activities in your area. Your puppy needs regular opportunities to play with other young dogs so she becomes a well-adjusted and sociable adult. Waiting for her to grow up before letting her have contact with other dogs does not work. If the breeder knows of a puppy club which offers puppy "play dates," then it would be a good idea make use of them. Your puppy has a lot to learn, so while she is playing with other dogs, do not interrupt unless one of the dogs becomes aggressive.

EXTRA

8-Step Guide to Housebreaking

Puppies must learn where they can and cannot go to the bathroom. All puppies, whether male or female, squat when they urinate.

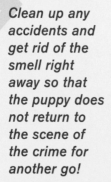

Clean up any accidents and get rid of the smell right away so that the puppy does not return to the scene of the crime for another go!

You want to housebreak your puppy but how do you go about this? She needs to learn where to go to the bathroom, but this does take time. Your puppy still does not yet understand where you want her to go, and you may also miss the signs that she needs to go. Observe her very carefully in the first few weeks, and whenever you think she is showing signs of needing to go to the bathroom, quickly take her to her newspapers, housebreaking pad, or out in the yard.

Step 1: Show Her Where to Go

The younger the puppy, the less understanding she will have of where to go to the bathroom. Just like a human baby, she needs time to learn where the right place to go is and you will need to show her this.

Step 2: Recognize When She Needs to Go

After sleeping and eating, a puppy soon needs to go to the bathroom. She may also need to go again fifteen minutes later. If she seems restless, appears to be searching for something, has an anxious facial expression, or she begins to squat, then she is about to go.

Step 3: Be Quick

Now it is up to you to react very quickly. The best thing to do is to pick her up. This will temporarily distract her, and she will not go to the bathroom while she is in your arms.

Step 4: Praise Her

Praise her for going to the bathroom in the correct place and give this action a phrase, such as "good pee pee, Sadie" or something similar. This way she will learn to go to the bathroom at your request.

Step 5: Do Not Pressure Her

Take it easy with her and wait patiently for her to go to the bathroom, if you think she needs to. Talk to her, praise her enthusiastically once she has done her business, and stroke her affectionately. Observe which places (in the yard) she decides to use each time.

Step 8: A Firm "No" Is Enough

If you catch your puppy going to the bathroom somewhere in the house, use a firm and resounding "no," and then carry her to the place she should go. If she finishes her business in the right place, praise her there. Do not push your puppy's nose into her feces or urine as

Step 6: Stay Outside for a While

If you immediately rush her inside after she has gone to the bathroom, your little puppy will soon get wise to this and hold it in so you have to wait. Do not underestimate her intelligence—dogs can be quite clever! Give her some time to sniff around and explore a bit, too.

punishment. This is cruel and will only make her afraid of you. She will not learn any faster by you doing this, so avoid any form of punishment at all costs.

When your puppy is playing, she might forget the right place to go to the bathroom.

Step 7: Bathroom Before Bedtime

Before she settles down for the night, take her out again. She should eventually be able to make it through the night without needing to go. But watch for any signs that she may need to go anyway.

This Is My Territory

After about six months of age, male dogs will begin to lift their leg when they urinate and will start to mark their territory by urinating several times on each walk, against trees, lampposts, fences, or benches. You cannot really stop him from doing this, but encourage him to keep walking if he is about to urinate on something he should not be marking.

Good Behavior
Training Principles

One of the most common words a puppy will hear when he is growing up is "No!"

An animal will not learn if he is stressed or anxious. Therefore, you should create a friendly, happy learning environment for your puppy so he learns quicker.

Every puppy must be trained. You will soon learn whether your puppy is naturally obedient or whether he tries to push boundaries. Training him gives you an excellent insight into his character. Is he a sensitive soul who just wants to please you, or is he a bit stubborn and full of mischief? Does he react to you saying "no" the first time? Or does he ignore you? After the tenth time you have said "no," is he still testing you out to see if you really mean it?

Time Alone

As long as you do not leave your puppy alone for too long, he will most likely doze until you get back and not get into trouble. Make sure your puppy is absolutely safe in his environment and feels secure with his new family before you leave him on his own for the first time. Test his reaction to your going out by taking the garbage out or getting the mail.

Patience

Every puppy will have a different reaction to being left on his own. Some readily accept it after a few days, but others need a few weeks to get used to it. Be patient and do not make a huge fuss over him before you leave. He may take this as a sign that your leaving is something to worry about. Your puppy needs to learn that everything is fine, and his humans will be home soon.

Greet Him Nicely

Always greet him in a friendly way when you return, even if he has done something naughty. Otherwise, he will connect you returning home with being scolded. Leave him somewhere cozy. Do not shut him in the bathroom, basement, or somewhere he does not have room to move!

Alone in the Car

Practice leaving him alone in the car for a short period of time; a car is a familiar space with windows he can look out of and see what is going on. If your mom or dad has stepped out to get a loaf of bread or you are being dropped off at school, ask your parents to take the puppy along so he can observe what is happening. Never leave your dog alone in the car for a long time on a hot day. He could suffer from heatstroke very quickly.

Take Your Puppy to Doggy School!

In order to get the best out of your four-legged friend, he will need to be trained. This applies to all dogs, even very small ones. Many dog clubs offer classes for puppies to socialize, learn, and play. With the right teacher, your dog will learn quickly and enjoy himself. Anyone can call himself or herself a dog trainer, so be careful and ask your parents to look for a trainer with the best teaching methods. Do not be afraid to have your parents ask the dog trainer about his or her qualifications and experience. Do not take your dog to a group which is not disciplined properly, or your puppy may end up being bullied by another dog. Playgroups should have the right mix of dogs and the right training methods.

Take your puppy to a puppy playgroup so he can get to know lots of other puppies and people, too.

What to Teach Your Puppy

Teaching your puppy to walk nicely on the leash is not always easy. If he pulls on his leash then make him stay still. Only keep walking once he has stopped pulling.

Your Puppy Learns in Three Ways

How does a dog learn? By observing, from experience, and through his natural willingness to please. He stores away whatever he sees in his memory and will avoid doing anything again that hurts or scares him. He is on the lookout for fun and also wants to please you. A dog is capable of learning many different tricks, and each breed has different abilities.

Leader of the Pack

A puppy has already learned to submit to his mother and siblings. Almost every puppy has a natural willingness to learn and follow his pack leader. Now you are the leader of the pack in his eyes.

On a Leash

Puppies need to learn how to walk on a leash. A leash is of course a safety measure to keep him from harm, such as busy streets, stray cats, or unfriendly dogs. A puppy will tend to follow behind you at first, but he may soon get brave and start to try and pull you along! If he does, change direction or stand still. Teach him to wait and once he is still, praise him, then continue with the walk.

Every dog should learn to master "Sit," "Down," "Stay," and "Come." Practice these commands regularly and reward him with praise and treats.

Sit

This short, simple word is easily understood by a puppy. Long sentences such as "Sit down now, please" are completely impossible for him to understand. If you say "Sit" and hold a treat in front of his nose, the puppy will automatically learn to sit, and will soon be doing this without treats in front of him.

Down

Hold a treat in your hand just above the ground and pull it away a small distance from the puppy. He will lower himself to the floor to reach the treat, and when he does this, immediately give him the treat and praise him.

Come

Your puppy may have already learned "Come" from the breeder whenever it was dinnertime. Say his name, plus the word *come* in a loud singsong voice. Give him a treat when he comes to you, and he will automatically connect this command with something tasty. Practice this exercise from time to time while you are out walking him.

Stay

Teach your puppy to remain sitting or lying down by saying "Stay," and then make him come to you on command. At first, this should only be over a very short distance, such as a few feet away from you. Then you can slowly increase this distance. You may need a second person to help you with this trick.

→ The Most Common Training Errors

→ 1. Expecting Perfection

Do not grumble at your puppy if he does not run in a straight line to you. After all, he did do what you said, even if he took the long way around. He will associate your grumbling with his action, which is coming over to you! The next time he might be reluctant or uninterested. So always be friendly and enthusiastic when he comes to you!

→ 2. Making It Too Hard

Call your puppy to you when he is coming toward you anyway, then you will have a better chance of teaching him what you want him to do. Practice the command "Come" when he is already on a leash, and then make your command louder if you need to.

→ 3. Praise for No Reason

When you praise him, be genuinely happy and excited. Dogs hear "wrong" notes and immediately get the wrong message. When you say "No," say it like you really mean it, be consistent, and only praise him when he has done something right. Otherwise, he will get confused.

→ 4. Give Chase

Do not run after him. He should be following you! Also stop him from chasing children, runners, and cyclists.

→ 5. Never . . .

Never ever use physical force to train your dog. Do not use electric collars, hit him, or scream at him. All these things will harm him, destroy any trust he has in you, and often he will not understand what he did wrong anyway.

Living alone on a deserted island is not our day-to-day reality. Both humans and dogs have to deal with densely populated habitats in the modern world and all the rules that go along with this. Otherwise, there will be trouble. Your puppy will have contact with people, other pets, wild animals, parks, sidewalk cafés, and many other things. You should take her training very seriously, or you will find yourself having to leave your dog at home because "she is just too much trouble."

Puppies and other animals will greet each other very cautiously. Each animal should carefully learn to understand the ways of the other.

People Friendly

Get your puppy used to the friendly pats from strangers and dog enthusiasts. Do not be upset when she runs joyfully to other people! This is a good thing and means that she is well socialized, including when she is around children. Under no circumstances should she ever snap at strangers.

Over the Top

Do you have a puppy who bounds enthusiastically over to children and strangers and is not frightened of anyone or anything? You will need to lay down some ground rules, or she could get herself into trouble. Put her on the leash, or distract her with a toy or treat. If she is some distance away from you and does not respond to your command to "Come!" said in a friendly but firm tone, then try turning on your heel and walking away. If she notices you walking away, she should hurry to catch up with you. But if she is not paying you any attention whatsoever and is hassling someone else, this is where the trouble could start. Unfortunately this might happen quite a bit at first. Apologize to the person and explain that your puppy is still very young and in the process of being trained.

Pick Up Her Waste

Always carry a plastic bag with you when you take your dog out. It is inconsiderate and in many places illegal to leave your dog's waste behind. When you pick up her feces, the warmth of it through the bag may feel absolutely disgusting to you, but you will soon get used to it and realize that none of it got on your hands! If your dog is very large, one bag may not be sufficient, so bring two just in case. You can buy dog-waste bags from any pet supply store or supermarket. These fit nicely into pockets, unlike big bulky plastic shopping bags that may have holes in them! If you cannot find a trash can, then you will have to carry the feces-filled bag back with you and properly dispose of it at home.

Is your dog very lively and enthusiastic with everyone she meets? Train her not to jump up at people because this makes some people very angry.

Curb Her Prey Drive

It is very important that your puppy learns not to chase ducks in the park, wild rabbits, deer in the forest, or the neighbor's cat. The same goes for joggers and cyclists. Make it clear to her that this is an absolute no-no. Unless she is running around in a fenced-in yard, she should always be on a leash. Do not forget to praise her when she is being obedient! Remember, the better the bond with your puppy, the greater your influence on her will be. You will need to nip any problems in the bud right away.

Spending time with dog buddies is an absolute must. Dogs learn through play.

Understanding and Training Your Puppy

The First Outing

→ Go on short walks only.

→ Do not ride your bike with your dog attached to it.

→ Depending on the breed, healthy young dogs do not usually need to wear protective clothing in cold or wet weather. Just keep him moving and do not stay out too long.

→ Dry your puppy thoroughly with a towel after he has been out in the rain.

→ Do not leave your dog outside in the rain or the cold.

Phases of Development

by Eberhard Trumler

1st and 2nd week:	vegetative phase
3rd week:	transition phase
4th to 8th week:	formative phase
8th to 12th week:	socialization period
12th to 18th week:	environmental socialization
13th to 16th week:	ranking order phase
5th to 6th month:	pack order phase
6th to 18th month:	puberty/sexual maturity
18th month to 3 years:	reaching adulthood

Stress-Free in Public

The best way to train your dog to behave well in public places:

→ Learn what to do from a good trainer

→ Socialize your dog with lots of different people

→ Obey leash rules in public

→ Pick up your dog's waste

→ Curb your puppy's prey drive

→ Do not allow your dog to jump on people

→ Put your dog on a leash when in large crowds

Dog Sports

Once your puppy is a year old and has healthy joints, he may enjoy participating in sports classes. You could involve him in basic training, agility, disc dog, obedience, dog tournaments, flyball (team sports), or in winter, dog sled sports or skijoring, which is where a dog pulls a person on skis. For more information, go online to research activities in your area you can do with your dog.

Words to Teach Your Dog

Your dog's name – So he looks up and waits to see what you expect of him.

Come! Here! – He should come running.

Stop! – So that he stops what he is doing.

Sit! Down! Stay! – He should sit, lie down, and not move from his spot.

Heel! – Train him to walk beside you.

Wait! – He should stay and wait for you.

Go pee! – Encourage him to urinate in a certain place.

Good dog! – Praise him when he does something right.

Translated from the German edition by Claire Mullen.

Edited and produced by Enslow Publishers, Inc.

Originally published in German.

© 2007 Franckh-Kosmos Verlags-GmbH & Co. KG,
    Stuttgart, Germany
    Brigitte Harries, *Welpe*

Library of Congress Cataloging-in-Publication Data

Harries, Brigitte.
    [Welpe. English]
    Puppies : keeping and caring for your pet / Brigitte Harries.
        pages cm. — (Keeping and caring for your pet)
    Includes bibliographical references and index.
    Summary: "Discusses how to choose and care for a puppy, including diet, training, behaviors, housing, grooming, exercise, and vet care"—Provided by publisher.
    ISBN 978-0-7660-4187-5
    1. Puppies—Juvenile literature. I. Title.
    SF426.5.H367 2013
    636.7'07—dc23
                                    2012038637

Paperback ISBN 978-1-4644-0305-7

Printed in the United States of America

052013 Lake Book Manufacturing, Inc., Melrose Park, IL

10 9 8 7 6 5 4 3 2 1

To Our Readers: We have done our best to make sure all Internet addresses in this book were active and appropriate when we went to press. However, the author and publisher have no control over and assume no liability for the material available on those Internet sites or on other Web sites they may link to. Any comments or suggestions can be sent by e-mail to comments@enslow.com or to the address on the back cover.

Every effort has been made to locate all copyright holders of material used in this book. If any errors or omissions have occurred, corrections will be made in future editions of this book.

All information in this book is given to the best of the author's knowledge. However, care during implementation is still required. The publishers, authors, and translators assume no liability for personal injury, property damage, or financial loss as a result of the application of the methods and ideas presented in this book.

♻ Enslow Publishers, Inc., is committed to printing our books on recycled paper. The paper in every book contains 10% to 30% post-consumer waste (PCW). The cover board on the outside of each book contains 100% PCW. Our goal is to do our part to help young people and the environment too!

Photo Credits: Color photos taken by Ulrike Schanz especially for the purposes of this book except Juniors Bildarchiv, p. 4 (left); Shutterstock.com, p. 1; Sabine Stuewer, p. 40; Sabine Stuewer/KOSMOS, pp. 66, 67.

Cover Photos: All from Shutterstock.com except author photo (back) by Ulrike Schanz. *Main photo:* papillon. *Bottom, left to right:* pug, Labrador retriever, Pomeranian, shih tzu. *Back:* German shepherd.

Index

Further Reading

Internet Addresses

American Kennel Club
http://www.akc.org

ASPCA: Dog Care
http://www.aspca.org/Home/
Pet-care/dog-care

Animal Planet: Dog Care 101
http://animal.discovery.com/
guides/dogs/caring/caring.html

Books

Arrowsmith, Claire, and Alison Smith. *Puppy Bible: The Ultimate Week-by-Week Guide to Raising Your Puppy.* Richmond Hill, Ontario, Canada: Firefly Books, 2013.

How to Housetrain Your Puppy in 14 Days or Less: The Complete Guide to Training Your Dog. Ocala, Fla.: Atlantic Publishing Group, Inc., 2012.

Morgan, Diane. *Complete Guide to Dog Breeds: Everything You Need to Know to Choose the Right Dog for You.* Neptune City, N.J.: TFH Publications, Inc., 2013.

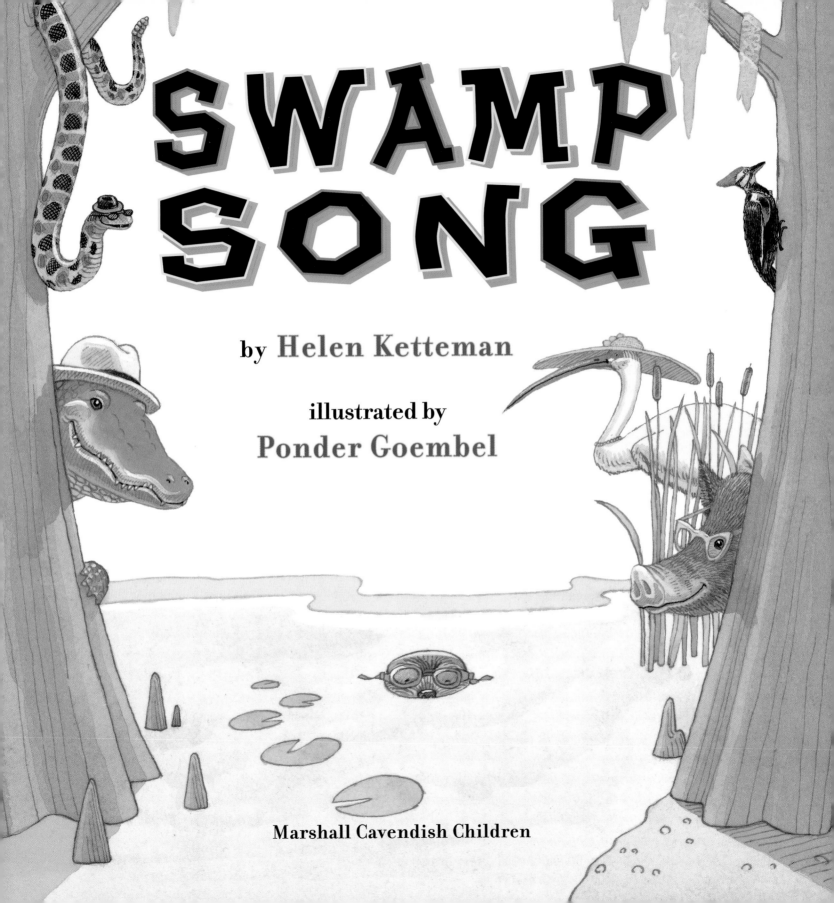

SWAMP SONG

by Helen Ketteman

illustrated by
Ponder Goembel

Marshall Cavendish Children

For sisters Crissy, Mary Ann, Jackie,
and Linda, with lots of love
—H.K.
To the children of the Riegelsville Library
—P.G.

Text copyright © 2009 by Helen Ketteman
Illustrations copyright © 2009 by Ponder Goembel

All rights reserved
Marshall Cavendish Corporation, 99 White Plains Road, Tarrytown, NY 10591
www.marshallcavendish.us/kids

Library of Congress Cataloging-in-Publication Data
Ketteman, Helen.
Swamp song / by Helen Ketteman ; illustrated by Ponder Goembel. — 1st ed.
p. cm.
Summary: Down in the swamp where the cypress grows, the animals all come out to enjoy the day.
ISBN 978-0-7614-5563-9
[1. Stories in rhyme. 2. Swamp animals — Fiction. 3. Swamps — Fiction.] I. Goembel, Ponder, ill. II. Title.
PZ8.3.K46Sw 2009
[E]— dc22
2008013810

The illustrations are colored ink lines with acrylic wash paint.
Book design by Anahid Hamparian
Editor: Marilyn Mark

Printed in Malaysia
First edition
1 3 5 6 4 2
mc Marshall Cavendish
Children

Down in the swamp
where the cypress grows,
Old Man Gator
starts tappin' his toes.
With a tip, tap, tippity-tap,

TIP, TAP, TAP.

Ibis stands
at the cattail hedge,
flappin' her wings
at the water's edge.

With a flip, flap, flippity-flap,

FLIP, FLAP, FLAP.

River Otter
swims with a swish,
splashin' the water
and chasin' the fish.
With a splish, splash, splishity-splash,

SPLISH, SPLASH, SPLASH.

Bullfrog hops
on a lily pad,
blowin' his throat
singin', "I'm so bad!"
With a crick, croak, crickity-croak,

CRICK, CROAK, CROAK.

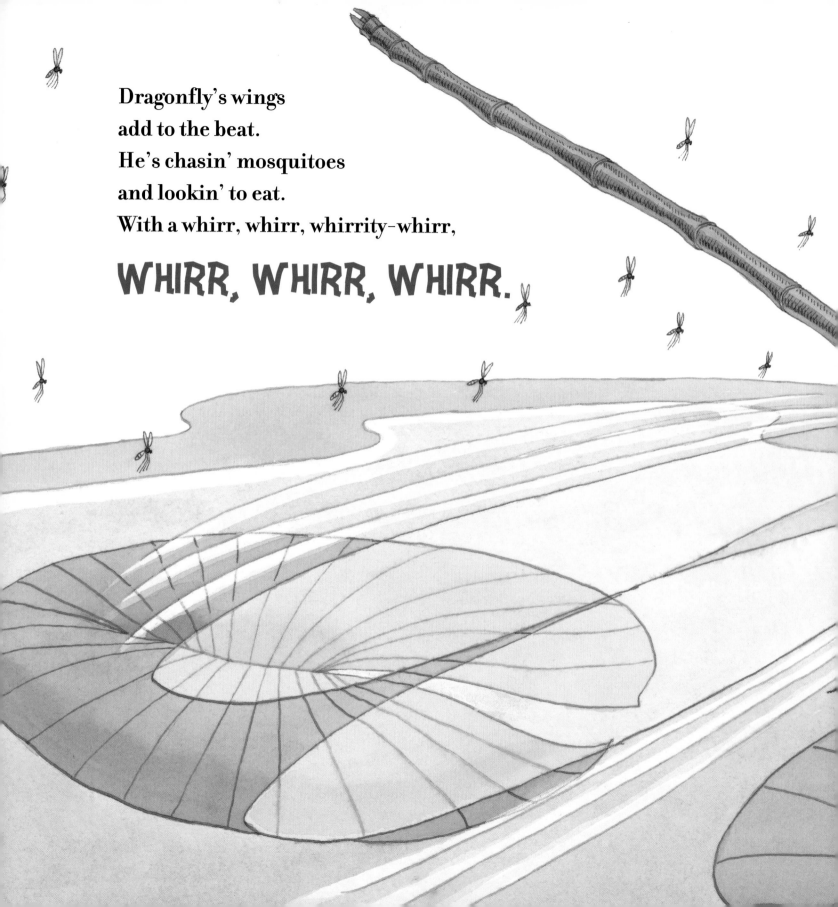

Dragonfly's wings
add to the beat.
He's chasin' mosquitoes
and lookin' to eat.
With a whirr, whirr, whirrity-whirr,

WHIRR, WHIRR, WHIRR.

Red Fox brings
her kits for a sip
and warns of gator
with a yippity-yip.
With a yip, yip, yippity-yip,
YIP, YIP, YIP.

Woodpecker knocks
on a tall slash pine,
searchin' for bugs
and lookin' to dine.
With a pick, peck, pickity-peck,

PICK, PECK, PECK.

Pygmy Rattler
slips through the sand,
shakin' his rattles
in beat with the band.
With a bizz, buzz, bizzity-buzz,

BIZZ, BUZZ, BUZZ.

Black Bear claws
at a cypress tree,
markin' his space
for all to see.
With a scritch, scratch, scritchity-scratch,

SCRITCH, SCRATCH, SCRATCH.

Wood Stork flutters
down from her nest,
clackin' her bill
and puffin' her chest.
With a click, clack, clickity-clack,

CLICK, CLACK, CLACK.

Fox Squirrel sits
on a cypress knee,
fuss, fuss, fussin'
as bold as can be.
With a chit, chee, chittery-chee,

CHIT, CHEE, CHEE.

Moorhen wades
on short red legs,
callin' her chicks
near the water's edge.
With an ack, ack, ackity-ack,

ACK, ACK, ACK.

Wild Boar leans
on an old tree stump,
then rubs back and forth
just scratchin' her rump.
With a grunt, grunt, grumpity-grunt,

GRUNT, GRUNT, GRUNT.

The music plays
all day long.
Each critter adds
to the swampy song:

CHITTERY-CHEE,

SPLISHITY-SPLASH,

CRICKITY-CROAK,

CLICKITY-CLACK,

PICKITY-PECK,

YIPPITY-YIP,

ACKITY-ACK,

And Old Man Gator
keeps tappin' his toes,
down in the swamp
where the cypress grows.

TIP, TAP, TIPPITY-TAP,
TIP, TAP, TAP.